GOOFY JOKES

By
Daryle Conners

SCHOLASTIC

◾SCHOLASTIC
www.scholastic.com

Published by Scholastic Inc., 557 Broadway, New York, NY 10012

Scholastic and associated logos are trademarks of Scholastic Inc.

Goofy Jokes is produced by becker&mayer!
11120 NE 33rd Place, Suite 101,
Bellevue, WA 98004
www.beckermayer.com

If you have questions or comments about this product, please visit www.beckermayer.com/customerservice.html and click on the Customer Service Request Form.

Edited by Betsy Henry Pringle
Designed by Rosanna Brockley
Design assistance by Greg Cook and Bryan Murphy
Photo research by Katie del Rosario
Production management by Diane Ross

Printed, manufactured, and assembled in Hangzhou, China 05/12
Conforms with CPSIA and ASTM standards F963-09.

10 9 8 7 6 5 4 3 2 1

ISBN: 978-1-60380-256-7

12116

Snort!

What's funnier than a giant schnoz? How about a giant schnoz you can use to sharpen pencils! The pencil sharpener on the cover of this book comes off, so you can gross out your teacher (or your parents) in style.

Carefully peel off and discard the plastic blister covering the nose, remove the pencil sharpener, insert your favorite pencil into the nose's right nostril, and rotate it!

Now that the hard work is done,sit back and enjoy goofy jokes that are guaranteed to make you groan, gag, giggle, or snort.

Q: Why was the nose so tired?

A: Because it had been running all day.

Q: What does a rain cloud wear under his raincoat?

A: Thunderware!

Teacher: Why is your homework in your father's handwriting?

Student: I borrowed his pen!

Q: Where do books sleep?

A: Under their covers!

Q: Why are pirates *pirates*?

A: Because they just arrrr!

Q: Why aren't elephants allowed on the beach?

A: They can't keep their trunks up!

Q: Why was Cinderella such a bad football player?

A: She had a pumpkin for a coach.

Q: What did the snowman's friends sing at his birthday?

A: "Freeze a Jolly Good Fellow!"

Knock, knock!

Who's there?

Radio.

Radio who?

Radio not, here I come!

Q: What did one pickle say to the other?

A: You mean a great dill to me.

Q: Which animal talks the most?

A: A yak!

Q: What room do ghosts avoid?

A: The living room.

Patient: Doctor, doctor! I think I'm a goat!

Doctor: How long has this been going on?

Patient: Ever since I was a kid.

Q: How do vampires like their food served?

A: In bite-size pieces.

Q: Why do seagulls live by the sea?

A: Because if they lived by the bay, they'd be bagels!

Knock, knock!

Who's there?

Cow go.

Cow go who?

No, cow go *moo!*

Q: What scary food lives at the beach?

A: A sandwitch!

Patient: Doctor, doctor! I feel like a deck of cards.

Doctor: I'll deal with you later!

Q: What did the hamburger give his sweetheart?

A: An onion ring!

Q: Where do crayons go on vacation?

A: Color-ado.

9

Q: What bird is always out of breath?

A: A puffin!

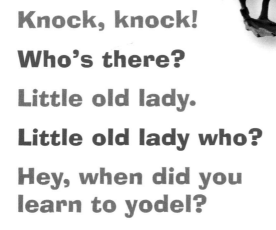

Knock, knock!

Who's there?

Little old lady.

Little old lady who?

Hey, when did you learn to yodel?

Q: What fruit always travels in groups of two?

A: Pears.

Q: Why didn't Superman know he could fly?

A: He didn't know his cape-abilities.

Q: What did Obi-Wan say to Anakin during the fancy banquet?

A: Use the forks!

Knock, knock!

Who's there?

Cash.

Cash who?

No, thanks.
I prefer peanuts.

Q: What kind of music do aliens like?

A: Nep-tunes.

Q: Where do cows go for fun?

A: The *moo*vies.

Q: How do you clean a dirty tuba?

A: With a tuba toothpaste!

Knock, knock!
Who's there?
Cargo.
Cargo who?
Cargo *beep, beep, VROOM!*

Q: How does bread stay warm?

A: With a breadspread!

Patient: Doctor, doctor!
I feel like a spoon.

Doctor: Sit over there and don't stir!

Q: How do monsters like their eggs?

A: Terri-fried!

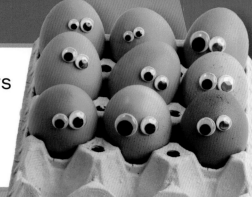

Q: What's orange and sounds like a parrot?

A: A carrot!

Q: What do elves make sandwiches with?

A: Shortbread!

Q: What's the difference between a teacher and a train?

A: One says, "Spit out your gum," and the other says, "Chew-chew!"

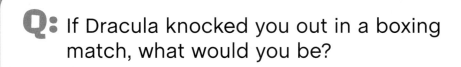

Q: If Dracula knocked you out in a boxing match, what would you be?

A: Out for the count!

Q: What does a martial arts fan eat?

A: Kung food!

Q: Why didn't the butterfly go to the dance?

A: Because it was a moth ball.

Q: Where was the Declaration of Independence signed?

A: At the bottom!

Q: What kind of garden does a baker have?

A: A flour garden!

Q: What animal has more lives than a cat?

A: A frog! He croaks every night.

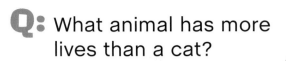

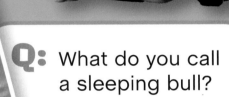

Q: What do you call a sleeping bull?

A: A bulldozer.

Q: What did the skeleton order at the restaurant?

A: Spare ribs!

Dad: The only way to learn a new skill is to start at the bottom.

Son: But I want to learn to swim!

Q: Why would Snow White be a good judge?

A: Because she's the fairest in the land

Q: Why did the football team go to the bank?

A: To get a quarter back!

Q: What kind of music does a blacksmith like?

A: Heavy metal!

Q: Why did the scientist put a knocker on his door?

A: Because he wanted the No-bell Prize.

Q: What do you call a 100-year-old ant?

A: An antique!

Q: How does the gingerbread man make his bed?

A: With cookie sheets.

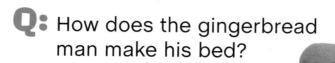

Snake 1: Are we poisonous?

Snake 2: Why do you ask?

Snake 1: I just bit my tongue!

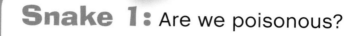

Q: Why did the pony cough?

A: He was a little horse.

Customer: Waiter, will my pizza be long?

Waiter: No sir, it will be round!

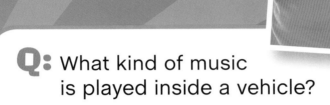

Q: What kind of music is played inside a vehicle?

A: Car-tunes!

Q: What did one shooting star say to another?

A: Glad to meteor!

Q: How much do pirates pay for their earrings?

A: A buccaneer!

Q: Why did the king go to the dentist?

A: To get a new crown!

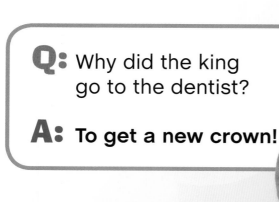

Q: How do you make a strawberry shake?

A: Tell it a scary story!

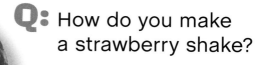

Q: How did the farmer fix his jeans?

A: With a cabbage patch!

Q: What game does Dr. Jekyll like best?

A: Hyde-and-seek!

Q: What do elves do after school?

A: Gnomework!

Knock, knock!

Who's there?

Tank.

Tank who?

You're welcome.

Q: Who invented fractions?

A: King Henry the 1/8!

Q: Why is Russia such a fast country?

A: Because the people are always Russian.

Q: Why did the chicken cross the playground?

A: To get to the other slide!

Q: What game makes the most noise?

A: Tennis—you can't play it without raising a racket!

Q: What is a volcano?

A: A mountain with hiccups!

Q: Why did King Arthur have a round table?

A: So no one could corner him.

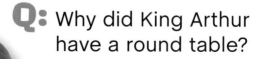

Q: How did the Vikings send secret messages?

A: By Norse code!

Q: Why don't anteaters get sick?

A: Because they are full of antibodies!

Q: If we breathe oxygen all day, what do we breathe all night?

A: Nitrogen!

Q: Why does a firefly glow?

A: It eats light meals.

Q: What happened to the man who plugged his electric blanket into a toaster?

A: He kept popping out of bed.

Q: Why was the chicken forbidden from sending e-mail?

A: Because she kept using fowl language.

Patient: Doctor, doctor! I keep thinking I'm a dog!

Doctor: Sit on the couch and we'll talk about it.

Patient: But I'm not allowed on the couch!

Q: When is a piece of wood like a king?

A: When it's a ruler!

Q: Why were the early days of history called the Dark Ages?

A: Because there were so many knights!

Q: Why did George Washington chop down the cherry tree?

A: I'm stumped!

Did you hear about the boy who wondered all night where the sun had gone?

It finally dawned on him.

Patient: Doctor, doctor! Everyone says I'm invisible.

Doctor: Who said that?

Q: What do you call cheese that belongs to someone else?

A: Nacho cheese!

29

Patient: Doctor, doctor!
I've just eaten 25 pancakes!

Doctor: Really? How waffle.

Q: Why couldn't Goldilocks sleep?

A: Nightbears.

Q: How do you make a hamburger smile?

A: Pickle it gently.

Knock, knock!
Who's there?
Alex Plane.
Alex Plane who?
Alex Plane later.

Q: Why do skeletons hate the cold?

A: The wind goes right through them!

Q: Where do burgers like to dance?

A: At a meatball!

Patient: Doctor, doctor! I feel like an electric eel.

Doctor: How shocking!

Q: What do you give a sick lemon?

A: Lemon aid!

Q: What did one slug say to the other?

A: I'll get you next slime.

Q: Which of the witch's friends eats the fastest?

A: The goblin.

Q: Why did the cookie go to the doctor?

A: It felt crummy.

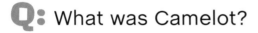

Q: What was Camelot?

A: A place where people parked their camels!

Q: Who do wizards stop for on the highway?

A: Witch-hikers.

Q: What do you call a cow's bedtime stories?

A: Dairy tales.

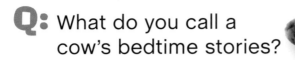

Customer:
Waiter, do you have frogs' legs?

Waiter:
No, sir, I've always walked like this.

Q: How does Yoda shave?

A: With a laser-blade.

Q: What do you call a man whose father was a cannon?

A: A son of a gun!

Q: What do you call a wizard from outer space?

A: A flying sorcerer!

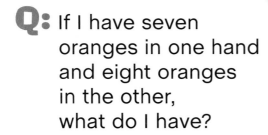

Q: If I have seven oranges in one hand and eight oranges in the other, what do I have?

A: Big hands!

Q: Do zombies eat popcorn with their fingers?

A: No. They eat the fingers separately.

Q: A knight wanted to be buried in his armor. What did it say on his tombstone?

A: Rust in peace.

Q: What did the balloon say to the pin?

A: Hi, Buster.

Q: What does a clam do on his birthday?

A: He shellebrates!

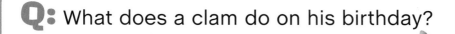

Camp Counselor: Eat your spinach.
It's good for growing kids.

Camper: Yeah, but who wants
to grow kids?

Q: How did the beaver get online?

A: He logged on.

Q: Why couldn't the pirate play cards?

A: Because he was standing on the deck.

Q: What lets you walk through walls?

A: Doors!

Q: What did the tree wear to the pool?

A: Swimming trunks!

Q: What does a frog do when its car breaks down?

A: It gets toad!

Q: Where should you put a noisy dog?

A: In a barking lot!

Q: What do cats call mice on skateboards?

A: Meals on wheels!

Q: What type of music are balloons scared of?

A: Pop music!

Q: What did Sir Lancelot wear to bed?

A: A knight gown.

Q: What did the doctor say to the shrinking man?

A: You'll just have to be a little patient.

Q: Where do you take a sick boat?

A: To the dock!

Q: What do snakes do after a fight?

A: They hiss and make up.

Q: How do you know if a clock is hungry?

A: It goes back four seconds.

Q: What is the most slippery country in the world?

A: Greece!

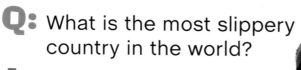

Customer: Waiter, this food tastes funny.

Waiter: Then why aren't you laughing?

Q: What is an archaeologist?

A: Someone whose career is in ruins.

Patient: Doctor, doctor!
My son just swallowed my pen
and I don't know what to do!

Doctor: **Use a pencil until I get
there.**

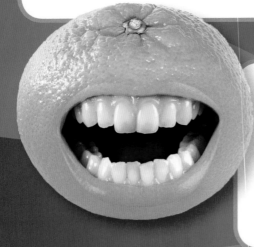

Q: Why did the man
stare at the can
of orange juice?

A: **Because it said
"concentrate."**

Q: What does a vegetarian zombie eat?

A: **Graaaaaaains!**

Q: What business is King Kong in?

A: **Monkey business.**

Q: What did the bee say to the flower?

A: Hello, honey!

Q: How can Mt. Everest hear everything you say?

A: Because it's covered with mountaineers.

Q: Why did Superman wrap himself in bread?

A: To make himself a hero sandwich!

43

Q: When do truck drivers stop to eat?

A: Whenever they come to a fork in the road.

Q: What did the first casket say to the second casket?

A: Is that you coffin?

Q: Who is braver, a stone or a tree?

A: The stone, because it's a little boulder.

Q: Where does smart butter go?

A: On the honor roll.

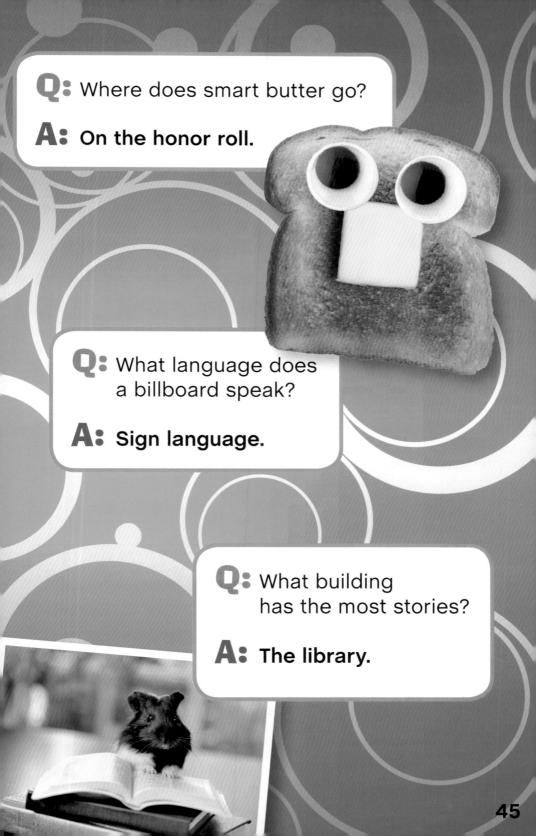

Q: What language does a billboard speak?

A: Sign language.

Q: What building has the most stories?

A: The library.

Q: Why did the belt go to jail?

A: For holding up a pair of pants.

Did you hear about the cat that swallowed a ball of wool?

She had mittens.

Q: What does a skeleton say before eating?

A: Bone appétit!

Q: What is a cheerleader's favorite cereal?

A: Cheerios!

Q: Why don't dogs make good dancers?

A: Because they have two left feet.

Q: Where can you learn to make ice cream?

A: In sundae school.

Q: What do you get when you cross a snowman with a vampire?

A: Frostbite.

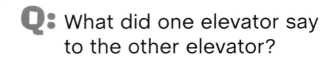

Q: What did one elevator say to the other elevator?

A: I think I'm coming down with something.

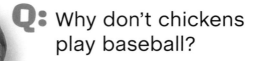

Q: Why don't chickens play baseball?

A: Because they hit fowl balls.

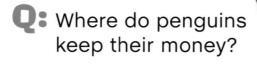

Q: Where do penguins keep their money?

A: In a snow bank!

48

Q: What do you call two witches who live together?

A: Broommates!

Q: Why did the vampire take art class?

A: He wanted to learn how to draw blood.

Q: Why did the clock get sick?

A: It was run down.

Q: What happened when the wheel was invented?

A: It caused a revolution!

Q: Where do generals keep their armies?

A: Up their sleevies!

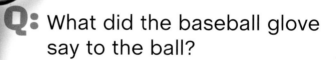

Q: What did the baseball glove say to the ball?

A: Catch you later.

Q: What do sea monsters eat for lunch?

A: Fish and ships.

Q: What lies at the bottom of the sea and shivers?

A: A nervous wreck.

Q: What is full of holes but can still hold water?

A: A sponge!

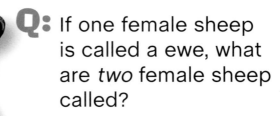

Q: If one female sheep is called a ewe, what are *two* female sheep called?

A: W!

Q: Why did the baseball coach hire a piano player?

A: Because he had perfect pitch!

Q: Where do baby ghosts go while their parents work?

A: To day scare!

Q: What do you call a happy cowboy?

A: A jolly rancher.

Q: What did the ocean say to the beach?

A: I'm not shore.

Q: What kinds of streets do zombies like?

A: Dead ends!

Q: What kind of shoes do spies wear?

A: Sneakers.

Q: What does a shark eat with peanut butter?

A: Jellyfish!

Q: Why can't a leopard hide?

A: Because he's always spotted!

Q: Why were the scouts so tired on April 1st?

A: They had just finished a 31-day March.

Q: Why are some fish at the bottom of the ocean?

A: Because they dropped out of school!

Q: What did one keyboard say to the other keyboard?

A: Sorry, you're not my type.

Q: How do you fix a broken tomato?

A: Tomato paste!

Q: Why did the baby strawberry cry?

A: His parents were in a jam.

Q: What did one math book say to the other math book?

A: Do you want to hear my problems?

Q: What tools do you need in math class?

A: Multi-pliers

Q: What did the dollar say to the four quarters?

A: You've changed!

Q: What is a vampire's favorite fruit?

A: A neck-tarine!

Q: How does the moon cut his hair?

A: E-clipse it!

Q: How do you get a baby astronaut to sleep?

A: You rock-it!

Q: What do you call Frosty the Snowman in the spring?

A: A puddle.

Q: What did the alien say to the book?

A: Take me to your reader.

EXTRA! EXTRA!
READ ALL ABOUT IT!
ALIENS
LAND!!!

Q: Why didn't the car feel well?

A: It had gas.

Q: What did the pen say to the pencil?

A: So, what's your point?

Q: How do you spot a modern spider?

A: She has a Web site.

Q: How did the barber win the race?

A: He knew a shortcut!

Q: Which part of a mermaid weighs the most?

A: The scales.

Q: What do you call it when your parachute doesn't open?

A: Jumping to a conclusion.

Q: What do you call a boomerang that doesn't work?

A: A stick.

Q: Why do the French like to eat snails?

A: Because they don't like fast food!

Q: What did the mountain climber name his son?

A: Cliff.

Q: What did the ocean say to the other ocean?

A: Nothing, they just waved.

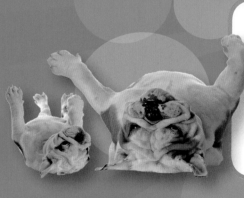

Q: Why was the dog kicked out of the flea circus?

A: Because he stole the show!

Q: What did Paul Revere say at the end of his famous ride?

A: Whoa!

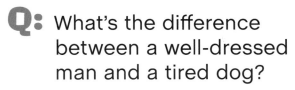

Q: What happened when the crooks fell in the ocean?

A: They started a crime wave.

Q: What's the difference between a well-dressed man and a tired dog?

A: One wears a suit, and the other just pants.

Q: What is the capital of Alaska?

A: Oh, come on—Juneau this one!

Q: What do you get when you cross a parrot with a centipede?

A: A walkie-talkie.

Q: What vegetable should you not take on a boat?

A: A leek!

Did you hear about the actor who fell through the floor?

It was just a stage he was going through.

Q: Why are opera singers good sailors?

A: **Because they can handle the high seas!**

Q: What do you get if a cement truck crashes into a jail?

A: **Hardened criminals.**

Patient: Doctor, doctor! I can't go to sleep!

Doctor: **Lie on the edge of the bed and soon you'll drop off.**

Q: Where do TVs go on vacation?

A: **To remote places.**